THE IRVING BERLIN FAKE BOOK

A Publication of

Irving Berlin Music Company®

EXCLUSIVELY DISTRIBUTED BY

7777 W. BLUEMOUND RD. P.O. BOX 13819 MILWAUKEE, WI 53213

Copyright © 1992 by HAL LEONARD PUBLISHING CORPORATION
International Copyright Secured   All Rights Reserved

For all works contained herein:
Unauthorized copying, arranging, adapting, recording or public performance is an infringement of copyright.
Infringers are liable under the law.

Irving Berlin logo and Irving Berlin Music Company are registered trademarks of the Estate of Irving Berlin.

ISBN 0-7935-1294-8

ALPHABETICAL LISTING

A

- 100 (Looking At You) Across The Breakfast Table
- 8 After You Get What You Want You Don't Want It
- 6 Alexander's Ragtime Band
- 8 All Alone
- 12 All By Myself
- 9 All Of My Life
- 7 Always
- 10 Any Bonds Today?
- 14 Anything You Can Do
- 13 At Peace With The World

B

- 16 Back To Back
- 11 Be Careful, It's My Heart
- 18 Because I Love You
- 18 Best Thing For You, The
- 15 Best Things Happen While You're Dancing, The
- 20 Better Luck Next Time
- 21 Blue Skies
- 19 But Where Are You?

C

- 26 Call Me Up Some Rainy Afternoon
- 17 Call Of The South, The
- 23 Change Partners
- 22 Cheek To Cheek
- 24 Colonel Buffalo Bill
- 26 Coquette
- 27 Count Your Blessings Instead Of Sheep
- 28 Couple Of Song And Dance Men, A
- 29 Couple Of Swells, A
- 30 (I'll See You In) Cuba

D

- 31 Doin' What Comes Natur'lly
- 37 Don't Be Afraid Of Romance
- 32 Don't Wait Too Long

E

- 33 Easter Parade
- 34 Empty Pockets Filled With Love
- 38 Everybody Knew But Me
- 36 Everybody Step
- 41 Everybody's Doin' It Now

F

- 40 Falling Out Of Love Can Be Fun
- 39 Fella With An Umbrella, A
- 42 Fools Fall In Love
- 45 For The Very First Time
- 44 Freedom Train, The

G

- 43 Gee, I Wish I Was Back In The Army
- 47 Get Thee Behind Me, Satan
- 46 Getting Nowhere (Running Around In Circles)
- 48 Girl On The Magazine Cover, The
- 49 Girl On The Police Gazette, The
- 50 Girl That I Marry, The
- 50 Give Me Your Tired, Your Poor
- 52 God Bless America

H

- 51 Happy Holiday
- 53 Harlem On My Mind
- 54 Heat Wave
- 56 Homework
- 58 Hostess With The Mostes' On The Ball, The
- 55 How About Me?
- 57 How Deep Is The Ocean (How High Is The Sky)
- 60 How Many Times?
- 61 How's Chances?

I

- 62 I Got Lost In His Arms
- 63 I Got The Sun In The Morning
- 64 I Keep Running Away From You
- 66 I Left My Heart At The Stage Door Canteen
- 68 I Love A Piano
- 67 I Never Had A Chance
- 69 I Say It's Spinach
- 70 I Used To Be Color Blind
- 71 I Want To Go Back To Michigan (Down On The Farm)
- 72 I'd Rather Lead A Band
- 65 I'll Capture Your Heart Singing
- 74 I'll Share It All With You
- 75 I'm A Bad, Bad Man
- 76 I'm Getting Tired So I Can Sleep
- 78 I'm Going Back To The Farm
- 77 I'm Playing With Fire
- 80 I'm Putting All My Eggs In One Basket
- 81 I'm Sorry For Myself
- 83 I've Got My Love To Keep Me Warm
- 82 If You Don't Want Me (Why Do You Hang Around)
- 85 Is He The Only Man In The World
- 84 Isn't This A Lovely Day (To Be Caught In The Rain?)
- 89 It Only Happens When I Dance With You
- 91 It's A Lovely Day Today
- 86 It's A Lovely Day Tomorrow

K

- 115 Kate (Have I Come Too Early, Too Late)

L

- 87 Lady Of The Evening
- 92 Lazy

93	Let Me Sing And I'm Happy	
94	Let Yourself Go	
95	Let's Face The Music And Dance	
88	Let's Have Another Cup O' Coffee	
96	Let's Start The New Year Right	
98	Let's Take An Old-Fashioned Walk	
97	Little Fish In A Big Pond	
90	Little Things In Life, The	
101	Louisiana Purchase	
102	Love And The Weather	
103	Love, You Didn't Do Right By Me	

M

104	Mandy
106	Manhattan Madness
105	Marie
108	Marrying For Love
109	Maybe It's Because I Love You Too Much
110	Me
111	Moonshine Lullaby
112	Mr. Monotony
114	My Defenses Are Down
116	My Walking Stick

N

118	No Strings (I'm Fancy Free)
117	Nobody Knows (And Nobody Seems To Care)
120	Now It Can Be Told

O

122	Oh! How I Hate To Get Up In The Morning
124	Old Fashioned Tune Always Is New, An
126	Old Fashioned Wedding, An
128	Only For Americans
121	Outside Of That I Love You

P

129	Paris Wakes Up And Smiles
130	Piccolino, The
132	Play A Simple Melody
134	Pretty Girl Is Like A Melody, A
135	Puttin' On The Ritz

R

119	Reaching For The Moon
136	Remember
133	Roses Of Yesterday
123	Russian Lullaby

S

163	Say It Isn't So
125	Say It With Music
131	Sayonara
137	Shaking The Blues Away
138	Sisters
139	Slumming On Park Avenue
141	Snookey Ookums
153	Soft Lights And Sweet Music
140	Some Sunny Day
155	Song Is Ended, The
142	Song Of Freedom
143	Steppin' Out With My Baby
144	Supper Time

T

145	Tell Me Little Gypsy
146	That International Rag
148	There's No Business Like Show Business
147	They Say It's Wonderful
150	This Is A Great Country
152	This Is The Army, Mr. Jones
151	This Year's Kisses
154	Top Hat, White Tie And Tails

W

156	Waiting At The End Of The Road
157	Waltz Of Long Ago, The
158	Washington Square Dance
149	Washington Twist
161	We Saw The Sea
160	We'll Never Know
164	What Chance Have I With Love
169	What'll I Do?
165	When I Leave The World Behind
166	When I Lost You
167	When The Midnight Choo-Choo Leaves For Alabam'
168	When Winter Comes
170	White Christmas
171	With My Head In The Clouds
172	With You

Y

173	You Can Have Him
174	You Can't Brush Me Off
176	You Can't Get A Man With A Gun
175	You Keep Coming Back Like A Song
180	You'd Be Surprised
181	You're Easy To Dance With
178	(I Wonder Why?) You're Just In Love
182	You're Laughing At Me
183	You're Lonely And I'm Lonely

CHRONOLOGICAL LISTING

YEARS 1910-1914

26	Call Me Up Some Rainy Afternoon	1910
6	Alexander's Ragtime Band	1911
41	Everybody's Doin' It Now	1911
166	When I Lost You	1912
167	When The Midnight Choo-Choo Leaves For Alabam'	1912
82	If You Don't Want Me (Why Do You Hang Around)	1913
141	Snookey Ookums	1913
146	That International Rag	1913
71	I Want To Go Back To Michigan (Down On The Farm)	1914
132	Play A Simple Melody	1914

YEARS 1915-1919

48	The Girl On The Magazine Cover	1915
68	I Love A Piano	1915
78	I'm Going Back To The Farm	1915
165	When I Leave The World Behind	1915
122	Oh! How I Hate To Get Up In The Morning	1918
104	Mandy	1919
117	Nobody Knows (And Nobody Seems To Care)	1919
134	A Pretty Girl Is Like A Melody	1919
180	You'd Be Surprised	1919

YEARS 1920-1924

8	After You Get What You Want You Don't Want It	1920
30	(I'll See You In) Cuba	1920
145	Tell Me Little Gypsy	1920
12	All By Myself	1921
36	Everybody Step	1921
125	Say It With Music	1921
87	Lady Of The Evening	1922
140	Some Sunny Day	1922
157	The Waltz Of Long Ago	1923
8	All Alone	1924
17	The Call Of The South	1924
92	Lazy	1924
169	What'll I Do?	1924

YEARS 1925-1929

7	Always	1925
32	Don't Wait Too Long	1925
136	Remember	1925
13	At Peace With The World	1926
18	Because I Love You	1926
60	How Many Times?	1926
160	We'll Never Know	1926
21	Blue Skies	1927
123	Russian Lullaby	1927
137	Shaking The Blues Away	1927
155	The Song Is Ended	1927
26	Coquette	1928
55	How About Me?	1928
93	Let Me Sing And I'm Happy	1928
105	Marie	1928
133	Roses Of Yesterday	1928
100	(Looking At You) Across The Breakfast Table	1929
135	Puttin' On The Ritz	1929
156	Waiting At The End Of The Road	1929
172	With You	1929

YEARS 1930-1934

90	The Little Things In Life	1930
110	Me	1931
153	Soft Lights And Sweet Music	1931
57	How Deep Is The Ocean (How High Is The Sky)	1932
69	I Say It's Spinach	1932
77	I'm Playing With Fire	1932
88	Let's Have Another Cup O' Coffee	1932
106	Manhattan Madness	1932
163	Say It Isn't So	1932
33	Easter Parade	1933
53	Harlem On My Mind	1933
54	Heat Wave	1933
61	How's Chances?	1933
109	Maybe It's Because I Love You Too Much	1933
119	Reaching For The Moon	1933
144	Supper Time	1933
67	I Never Had A Chance	1934

YEARS 1935-1939

22	Cheek To Cheek	1935
84	Isn't This A Lovely Day (To Be Caught In The Rain?)	1935
118	No Strings (I'm Fancy Free)	1935
130	The Piccolino	1935
154	Top Hat, White Tie And Tails	1935
19	But Where Are You?	1936
47	Get Thee Behind Me, Satan	1936
72	I'd Rather Lead A Band	1936
80	I'm Putting All My Eggs In One Basket	1936
94	Let Yourself Go	1936
95	Let's Face The Music And Dance	1936
161	We Saw The Sea	1936
49	The Girl On The Police Gazette	1937
83	I've Got My Love To Keep Me Warm	1937
139	Slumming On Park Avenue	1937
151	This Year's Kisses	1937

182	You're Laughing At Me	1937
23	Change Partners	1938
70	I Used To Be Color Blind	1938
116	My Walking Stick	1938
120	Now It Can Be Told	1938
16	Back To Back	1939
52	God Bless America	1939
81	I'm Sorry For Myself	1939
86	It's A Lovely Day Tomorrow	1939
124	An Old Fashioned Tune Always Is New	1939
168	When Winter Comes	1939

YEARS 1940-1944

42	Fools Fall In Love	1940
101	Louisiana Purchase	1940
121	Outside Of That I Love You	1940
164	What Chance Have I With Love	1940
174	You Can't Brush Me Off	1940
183	You're Lonely And I'm Lonely	1940
10	Any Bonds Today?	1941
11	Be Careful, It's My Heart	1942
51	Happy Holiday	1942
66	I Left My Heart At The Stage Door Canteen	1942
65	I'll Capture Your Heart Singing	1942
76	I'm Getting Tired So I Can Sleep	1942
96	Let's Start The New Year Right	1942
142	Song Of Freedom	1942
152	This Is The Army, Mr. Jones	1942
170	White Christmas	1942
171	With My Head In The Clouds	1942
181	You're Easy To Dance With	1942
175	You Keep Coming Back Like A Song	1943
9	All Of My Life	1944

YEARS 1945-1949

28	A Couple Of Song And Dance Men	1945
38	Everybody Knew But Me	1945
46	Getting Nowhere (Running Around In Circles)	1945
14	Anything You Can Do	1946
24	Colonel Buffalo Bill	1946
31	Doin' What Comes Natur'lly	1946
50	The Girl That I Marry	1946
62	I Got Lost In His Arms	1946
63	I Got The Sun In The Morning	1946
74	I'll Share It All With You	1946
75	I'm A Bad, Bad Man	1946
111	Moonshine Lullaby	1946
114	My Defenses Are Down	1946
148	There's No Business Like Show Business	1946
147	They Say It's Wonderful	1946
176	You Can't Get A Man With A Gun	1946
20	Better Luck Next Time	1947
29	A Couple Of Swells	1947
39	A Fella With An Umbrella	1947
44	The Freedom Train	1947
89	It Only Happens When I Dance With You	1947
115	Kate (Have I Come Too Early, Too Late)	1947
102	Love And The Weather	1947
112	Mr. Monotony	1947
143	Steppin' Out With My Baby	1947
98	Let's Take An Old-Fashioned Walk	1948
40	Falling Out Of Love Can Be Fun	1949
50	Give Me Your Tired, Your Poor	1949
56	Homework	1949
97	Little Fish In A Big Pond	1949
128	Only For Americans	1949
129	Paris Wakes Up And Smiles	1949
173	You Can Have Him	1949

YEARS 1950-1966

18	The Best Thing For You	1950
58	The Hostess With The Mostes' On The Ball	1950
91	It's A Lovely Day Today	1950
108	Marrying For Love	1950
158	Washington Square Dance	1950
178	(I Wonder Why?) You're Just In Love	1950
27	Count Your Blessings Instead Of Sheep	1952
45	For The Very First Time	1952
15	The Best Things Happen While You're Dancing	1953
103	Love, You Didn't Do Right By Me	1953
138	Sisters	1953
43	Gee, I Wish I Was Back In The Army	1954
64	I Keep Running Away From You	1957
131	Sayonara	1957
37	Don't Be Afraid Of Romance	1962
34	Empty Pockets Filled With Love	1962
85	Is He The Only Man In The World	1962
150	This Is A Great Country	1962
149	Washington Twist	1962
126	An Old Fashioned Wedding	1966

After You Get What You Want You Don't Want It

All Alone

ALL OF MY LIFE

Words and Music by
IRVING BERLIN

© Copyright 1944 by Irving Berlin
© Copyright Renewed

First came the Czechs and the came the Poles and then the Nor-we-gians with three mil-lion souls.

Then came the Dutch, the Bel-gians and France, then all of the Bal-kans with hard-ly a chance. It's

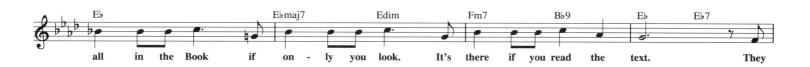
all in the Book if on-ly you look. It's there if you read the text. They

fell ev-'ry one at the point of a gun. A-mer-i-ca must-n't be next. An-y

BE CAREFUL, IT'S MY HEART
(From The Motion Picture Irving Berlin's HOLIDAY INN)

© Copyright 1942 by Irving Berlin
© Copyright Renewed

Words and Music by
IRVING BERLIN

Freely

Sweet-heart of mine, I've sent you a val-en-tine. Sweet-heart of mine,

it's more than a val-en-tine. Be care-ful, it's my heart. It's

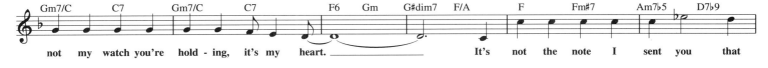
not my watch you're hold-ing, it's my heart. It's not the note I sent you that

you quick-ly burned. It's not the book I lent you that you nev-er re-turned. Re-

mem-ber, it's my heart. The heart with which so will-ing-ly I part.

It's yours to take to keep or break, but please, be-fore you start, be care-ful,

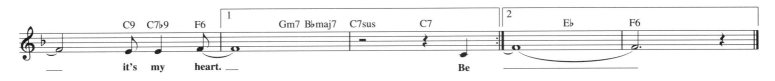
it's my heart. Be

AT PEACE WITH THE WORLD

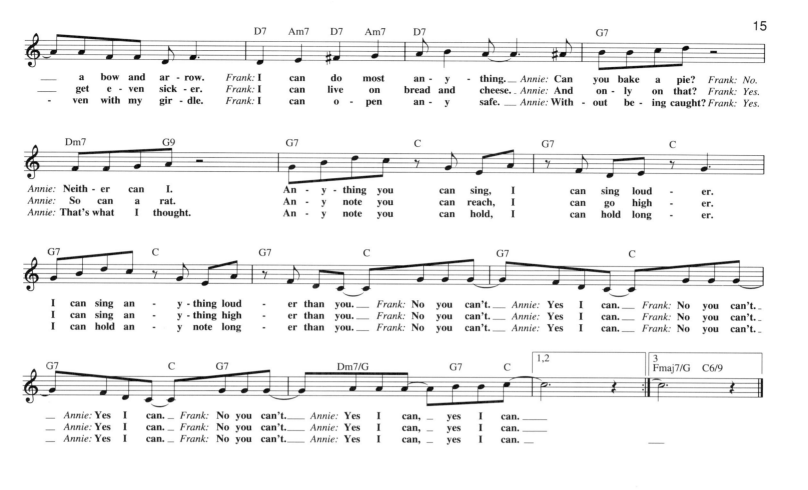

THE BEST THINGS HAPPEN WHILE YOU'RE DANCING
(From The Motion Picure Irving Berlin's WHITE CHRISTMAS)

© Copyright 1953 by Irving Berlin
© Copyright Renewed

Words and Music by
IRVING BERLIN

18

BECAUSE I LOVE YOU

© Copyright 1926 by Irving Berlin
© Copyright Renewed

Words and Music by
IRVING BERLIN

THE BEST THING FOR YOU
(From The Stage Production CALL ME MADAM)

© Copyright 1950 by Irving Berlin
© Copyright Renewed

Words and Music by
IRVING BERLIN

Better Luck Next Time
(From The Motion Picture Irving Berlin's EASTER PARADE)

Words and Music by IRVING BERLIN

© Copyright 1947, 1948 by Irving Berlin
© Copyright Renewed

Blue Skies

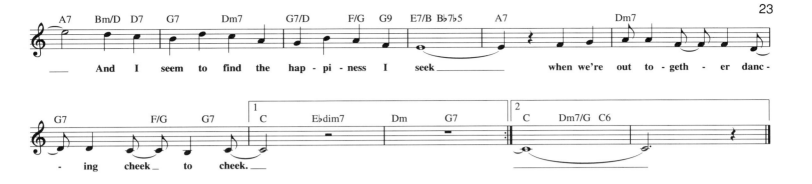

Call Me Up Some Rainy Afternoon

Words and Music by
IRVING BERLIN

© Copyright 1910 by Irving Berlin
© Copyright Renewed

Moderately

Nel - lie Green met Har - ry Lee, at a mas-quer-ade the oth - er night. He like she, and
He look'd wise, then looked for rain, sure e-nough it rained that Sat - ur-day. "Give me three, four,

she liked he, just a case of love at sin - gle sight. He took Nel - lie home that eve,
five, six Main, Nel - lie dear, pre-pare I'm on my way." When he rang the front door bell,

al - so took the num - ber of her phone. Just be - fore he took his leave, Nel - lie whis-pered in the cut - est
no one there re-spond - ed to his call. Soon he heard his pret - ty Nell, sing - ing to some-bod - y in the

tone. } Call me up some rain - y aft - er - noon, I'll ar - range for a qui - et lit - tle spoon. Think of
hall. }

all the joy and bliss, we can hug and we can talk a - bout the weath - er. We can have a qui - et lit - tle

talk. I will see that my moth - er takes a walk. Mum's the word when we meet, be a

To Coda ⊕   1   2   CODA ⊕
mas - on, don't re-peat. An - gel eyes are you wise? Good - bye.   Call me, bye.   D.C. al Coda   bye.

COQUETTE
(From The Motion Picture COQUETTE)

Words and Music by
IRVING BERLIN

© Copyright 1928 by Irving Berlin
© Copyright Renewed

Moderately

Just a sweet co - quette, so they say and yet I know how true you can be.
Now that I love you, and you love me too I'll keep you close to my heart.

Just a but - ter - fly, so they say but I know just how much you love me.
Now that I can see you be - long to me; noth - ing can keep us a - part.

The oth - ers you've met may call you Co - quette, but I'll al - ways call you

COUNT YOUR BLESSINGS INSTEAD OF SHEEP
(From The Motion Picture Irving Berlin's WHITE CHRISTMAS)

Words and Music by
IRVING BERLIN

© Copyright 1952 by Irving Berlin
© Copyright Renewed

A COUPLE OF SWELLS
(From The Motion Picture Irving Berlin's EASTER PARADE)

DON'T WAIT TOO LONG

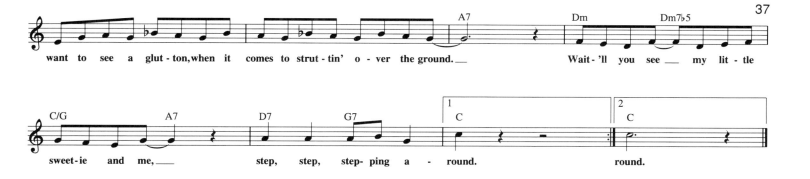

DON'T BE AFRAID OF ROMANCE
(From The Stage Production MR. PRESIDENT)

Words and Music by
IRVING BERLIN

© Copyright 1962 by Irving Berlin
© Copyright Renewed

A FELLA WITH AN UMBRELLA
(From The Motion Picture Irving Berlin's EASTER PARADE)

Words and Music by
IRVING BERLIN

Medium slow

Who am I, what's my name, where I'm from, how I came, does-n't mat-ter, dear. 'Long as I am here.

Moderately, with a lilt

(Male:) I'm just a fel-la, a fel-la with an um-brel-la, look-ing for a girl who saved her love for a rain-y day. I'm just a fel-la, a fel-la with an um-brel-la, glad to see the skies of blue have turned in-to skies of gray.

(Female:) I met a fel-la, a fel-la with an um-brel-la, look-ing for a girl who saved her love for a rain-y day. I met a fel-la, a fel-la with an um-brel-la, wait-ing for the skies of blue to turn in-to skies of gray.

Rain-drops have brought us to-geth-er and that's what I longed to see. May-be the break in the weath-er will prove to be a break for me. So I'll be the fel-la, the fel-la with an um-brel-la, if you'll be the girl who saved her love for a rain-y day.

Rain-drops will bring us to-geth-er and that's what I long to see. May-be a break in the weath-er will prove to be a break for me. For I told the fel-la, the fel-la with the um-brel-la, I could be the girl who saved her love for a rain-y day.

© Copyright 1947, 1948 by Irving Berlin
© Copyright Renewed

Falling Out Of Love Can Be Fun
(From The Stage Production MISS LIBERTY)

© Copyright 1949 by Irving Berlin
© Copyright Renewed

Words and Music by
IRVING BERLIN

Moderately

Croc-o-dile tears will not be shed, they're not for a la-dy like I'm. I can re-call what my aunt said when she mar-ried for the twen-ti-eth time.

Fall-ing out of love can be fun. ___
Fall-ing out of love can be fun. ___

af-ter love is o-ver and done. ___ It's an aw-ful blow but al-though ___ it's up-set-ting.
some-one else may soon be the one. ___ By an-oth-er name he's the same ___ as his broth-er.

So much you can do ___ while you're for-get-ting fall-ing out of love can be fun. ___
Close your eyes and one ___ is like the oth-er, fall-ing out of love can be fun. ___

When you find your lov-er has gone ___ get your sec-ond wind and go on. ___
If he leaves you af-ter you've wed ___ and the stork is o-ver your head. ___

There's an old af-fair that is there ___ for re-new-ing. In your grief do you ___ know what you're do-ing. Fall-
Soon you're gon-na be with a she ___ or a lad-die. Smile as you go shop-ping for a dad-dy. Fall-

-ing out of love can be fun. ___ Soon you'll be swing-ing in a ham-mock on a porch.
-ing out of love can be fun. ___ Soon you'll be los-ing all your trou-bles and your fears.

One arm wrapped a-round some-one else. ___ The oth-er one car-ry-ing the
One eye wink-ing at some-one else. ___ The oth-er eye fill-ing up with

torch. Love can give a la-dy a clout ___ and she may be down but not out. ___
tears. When you find your lov-ing ro-mance ___ gets a sud-den kick in the pants. ___

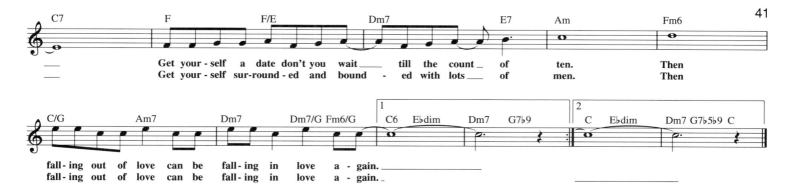

EVERYBODY'S DOIN' IT NOW

Words and Music by
IRVING BERLIN

© Copyright 1911 by Irving Berlin
© Arrangement Copyright 1955 by Irving Berlin
© Copyright Renewed

THE FREEDOM TRAIN

© Copyright 1947 by Irving Berlin
© Copyright Renewed by Irving Berlin
© Copyright Assigned to Joe DiMaggio, Anne Phipps Sidamon-Eristoff and
Theodore R. Jackson as Trustees of God Bless America Fund

Words and Music by
IRVING BERLIN

Moderately

This song is a train song. It's a song a-bout a train.
Not the Atch-i-son To-pe-ka, not the Chatt-a-noo-ga Choo-Choo,
nor the one that leaves at mid-night for the State of Al-a-bam'.
This song is a train song where the en-gin-eer is Un-cle Sam.
Here comes the free-dom train. You bet-ter hur-ry down
just like a Paul Re-vere. It's com-in' in-to your home town.
In-side the free-dom train you'll find a pre-cious freight.
Those words of lib-er-ty, the do-cu-ments that made us great.

You can shout your an-ger from a stee-ple. You can shoot the sys-tem full of holes.
You can write the Pre-si-dent a let-ter. You can ev-en tell him to his face.
You can hate the laws that you're o-bey-ing. You can shout your an-ger to the crowd.

You can al-ways quest-ion "We The Peo-ple." You can get your an-swer at the polls.
If you think that you can do it bet-ter, get the votes and you can take his place.
We may dis-a-gree with what you're say-ing, but we'll fight to let you say it loud.

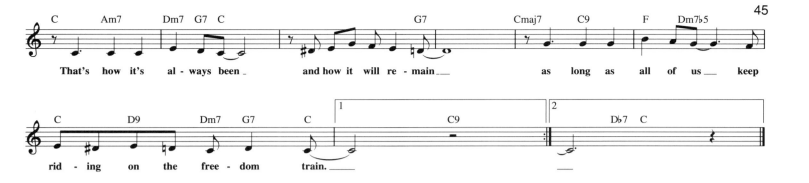

FOR THE VERY FIRST TIME

Words and Music by
IRVING BERLIN

© Copyright 1952 by Irving Berlin
© Copyright Renewed

GETTING NOWHERE (RUNNING AROUND IN CIRCLES)
(From The Motion Picture BLUE SKIES)

© Copyright 1945 by Irving Berlin
© Copyright Renewed

Words and Music by
IRVING BERLIN

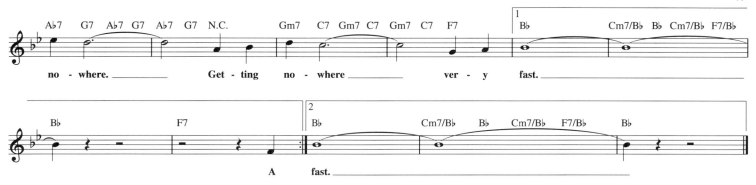

THE GIRL ON THE POLICE GAZETTE
(From The Motion Picture ON THE AVENUE)

Words and Music by
IRVING BERLIN

Slowly with expression

Some fellows see the girl that they love in a dream. Some fellows see their love in a rippling stream. I saw the girl that I can't forget, on the cover of a police gazette. If I could find her life would be peaches and cream. Oh my search will never cease for the girl on the police gazette. For the pretty young brunette on the pink police gazette. And above my mantle piece there's a page of the police gazette. With the pretty young brunette. On the pink police gazette, I love to stop at my fav-'rite barber shop. Just to take another look at the girl that I haven't met yet. And my longing will increase for the girl on the police gazette. For the pretty young brunette, on the pink police ga- zette. Oh my zette.

THE GIRL THAT I MARRY
(From The Stage Production ANNIE GET YOUR GUN)

GIVE ME YOUR TIRED, YOUR POOR
(From The Stage Production MISS LIBERTY)

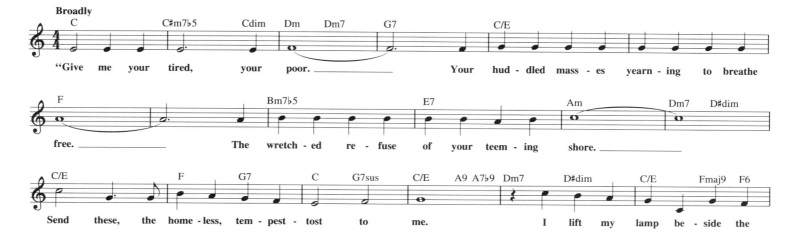

GOD BLESS AMERICA

© Copyright 1938, 1939 by Irving Berlin
© Copyright Renewed 1965, 1966 by Irving Berlin
© Copyright Assigned to Joe DiMaggio, Anne Phipps Sidamon-Eristoff and
Theodore R. Jackson as Trustees of God Bless America Fund

Words and Music by
IRVING BERLIN

While the storm clouds gath-er far a-cross the sea, let us swear al-le-giance to a land that's free. Let us all be grate-ful for a land so fair, as we raise our voi-ces in a sol-emn prayer. God bless A-mer-i-ca, land that I love. Stand be-side her and guide her thru the night with a light from a-bove. From the moun-tains, to the prai-ries, to the o-ceans white with foam. God bless A-mer-i-ca, my home sweet home. God bless A-mer-i-ca, my home sweet home. home.

HARLEM ON MY MIND
(From The Stage Production AS THOUSANDS CHEER)

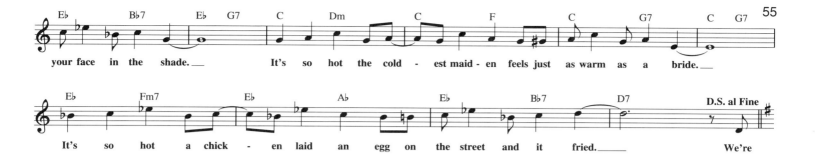

HOW ABOUT ME?

Words and Music by
IRVING BERLIN

© Copyright 1928 by Irving Berlin
© Arrangement Copyright 1956 by Irving Berlin
© Copyright Renewed

HOW DEEP IS THE OCEAN
(How High Is The Sky)

Words and Music by
IRVING BERLIN

HOW MANY TIMES?

© Copyright 1926 by Irving Berlin
© Copyright Renewed

Words and Music by
IRVING BERLIN

Moderately

A fel-low and his la-dy friend walk-ing ____ and talk-ing ____ of love. ____ A
A cer-tain thing has puz-zled me great-ly, ____ just late-ly, ____ my dear. ____ Why

moon that has a sil-ver-y lin-ing ____ is shin-ing ____ a-bove. ____ The
does a fel-low al-ways get stup-id ____ when Cu-pid ____ is near. ____ Al-

girl-ie says you cer-tain-ly do like ____ to coo like ____ a dove. ____ A
though I was the smart-est at col-lege, ____ that know-ledge, ____ I fear ____ could

ner-vous youth, ____ a jea-lous miss, ____ who want the truth ____ is ask-ing this: ____
nev-er bring ____ a Rom-e-o ____ the on-ly thing ____ he wants to know. ____

How man-y times ____ have you said, ____ "I love you?" ____ How man-y times ____

have you said, ____ "I'll be true?" ____ How man-y won-

-der-ful sweet-ies have you told that to? ____ How man-y times ____ has a

cer-tain feel-ing trou-bled you so ____ that you "hit the ceil-ing?" How man-y hands

have you held ____ all a-lone? ____ How man-y lips ____ have you pressed ____

to your own? ____ I'd hate to think that you kissed too man-y, but

I'd feel worse if you had-n't kissed an-y. Please tell me how ____ man-y times?

I GOT LOST IN HIS ARMS
(From The Stage Production ANNIE GET YOUR GUN)

Words and Music by
IRVING BERLIN

Moderately

Don't ask me just how it hap-pened, I wish I knew. I can't be-lieve that it's hap-pened, and still it's true. I got lost in his arms, and I had to stay. It was dark in his arms, and I lost my way. From the dark came a voice, and it seemed to say, "There you go. There you go." How I felt as I fell I just can't re-call. But his arms held me fast, and it broke the fall. And I said to my heart as it fool-ish-ly kept jump-ing all a-round, "I got lost but look what I found." I got

I GOT THE SUN IN THE MORNING
(From The Stage Production ANNIE GET YOUR GUN)

© Copyright 1946 by Irving Berlin
© Copyright Renewed

Words and Music by
IRVING BERLIN

Light Bounce

Tak-ing stock of what I have and what I have-n't, what do I find? The things I've got will keep me sat-is-fied. Check-ing up on what I have and what I have-n't, what do I find? A health-y bal-ance on the cred-it side.

Medium jump tempo

Got no dia-mond, got no pearl, still I think I'm a luck-y girl. I got the sun in the morn-ing and the moon at night. Got no man-sion, got no yacht, still I'm hap-py with what I've got. I got the sun in the morn-ing and the moon at night. Sun-shine gives me a love-ly day. Moon-light gives me the milk-y way. Got no check-books, got no banks, still I'd like to ex-press my thanks. I got the sun in the morn-ing and the moon at night. And with the sun in the morn-ing and the moon in the eve-ning, I'm all right.

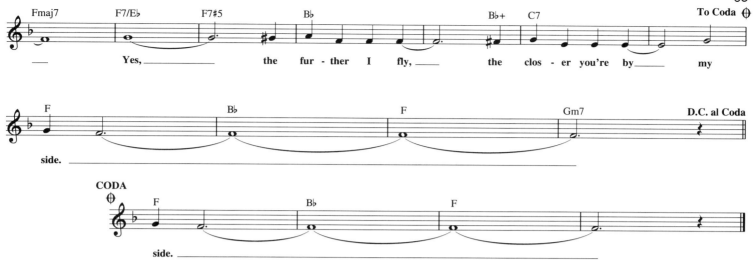

I'LL CAPTURE YOUR HEART SINGING
(From The Motion Picture Irving Berlin's HOLIDAY INN)

© Copyright 1942 by Irving Berlin
© Copyright Renewed

Words and Music by
IRVING BERLIN

I LEFT MY HEART AT THE STAGE DOOR CANTEEN
(From The Stage Production THIS IS THE ARMY)

Words and Music by
IRVING BERLIN

© Copyright 1942 by Irving Berlin
© Copyright Renewed by Irving Berlin
© Copyright Assigned to Joe DiMaggio, Anne Phipps Sidamon-Eristoff
and Theodore R. Jackson as Trustees of God Bless America Fund

Slowly

Old Mister Absent-minded, that's me. Just as forgetful as I can be. I've got the strangest sort of a mind. I'm always leaving something behind. I left my heart at the stage door canteen. I left it there with a girl named Eileen. I kept her serving doughnuts 'til all she had were gone. I sat there dunking doughnuts 'til she caught on. I must go back to the Army routine. And ev'ry doughboy knows what that will mean. A soldier boy without a heart has two strikes on him from the start and my heart's at the stage door canteen. I left my teen.

I SAY IT'S SPINACH
(From The Stage Production FACE THE MUSIC)

Words and Music by
IRVING BERLIN

I WANT TO GO BACK TO MICHIGAN
(DOWN ON THE FARM)

Words and Music by
IRVING BERLIN

© Copyright 1914 by Irving Berlin
© Copyright Renewed

Moderately

I was born in Michigan, and I wish and wish again that I was
You can keep your cabarets where they turn nights into days. I'd rather

back in the town where I was born. There's a farm in
be where they go to bed at nine. I've been gone for

Michigan, and I'd like to fish again in the river that
seven weeks, and I've lost my rosy cheeks. That's the reason I'd

flows beside the fields of waving corn. A lonesome soul am
rather have the country life for mine. My thoughts are far a-

I. Here's the reason why: I want to go back, I want to
way. That's just why I say:

go back, I want to go back to the farm. Far away from

harm, with a milk pail on my arm. I miss the rooster, the one that

"use-ter" wake me up at four a.m. I think your

great big city's very pretty. Nevertheless, I want to be there. I want to

see there a certain someone full of charm. That's why I wish again that

I was in Michigan down on the farm. I want to farm.

I'M GETTING TIRED SO I CAN SLEEP
(From The Stage Production THIS IS THE ARMY)

Words and Music by
IRVING BERLIN

I'M PLAYING WITH FIRE

© Copyright 1932 by Irving Berlin
© Copyright Renewed

Words and Music by
IRVING BERLIN

Moderately

I've heard a-bout you, each word a-bout you, that ev-'ry-one has spo-ken. And from the things I hear, I should be care-ful dear. They come and find me and then re-mind me of all the hearts you've bro-ken. But I'm in love with you. So what am I to do? I'm play-ing with fire, I'm gon-na get burned. I know it, but what can I do? I know my heart must be con-tent to go where it is sent, al-though I may re-pent when I'm through. But what can I do? I'm play-ing with fire I'm gon-na get burned while mer-ry-go-round-ing with you. But I go for my ride with my eyes o-pen wide. I'm play-ing with fire. I know it but, what can I do? do?

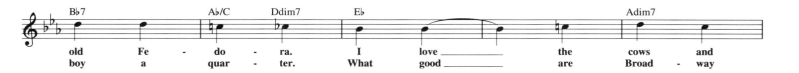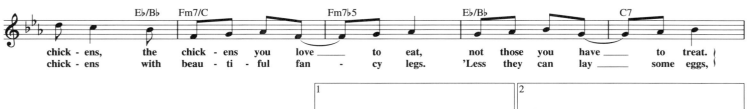

I'M SORRY FOR MYSELF
(From The Motion Picture Irving Berlin's SECOND FIDDLE)

Words and Music by
IRVING BERLIN

Additional Lyrics

4. So very blue am I;
   I wish that I could die.
   Wish I had a nasty cough,
   I'd buy a gun, but then it might go off.
   I'm so sorry for myself.

5. I soon could end my woes
   down where the river flows.
   I would jump right in the sea,
   but no one may be there to rescue me.
   I'm so sorry for myself.

IT'S A LOVELY DAY TOMORROW
(From The Stage Production LOUISANA PURCHASE)

© Copyright 1939 by Irving Berlin
© Copyright Renewed

Words and Music by
IRVING BERLIN

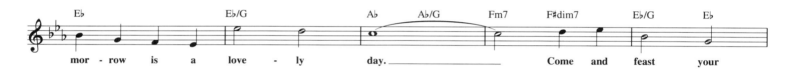

Lady of the Evening
(From The 1922 Stage Production MUSIC BOX REVUE)

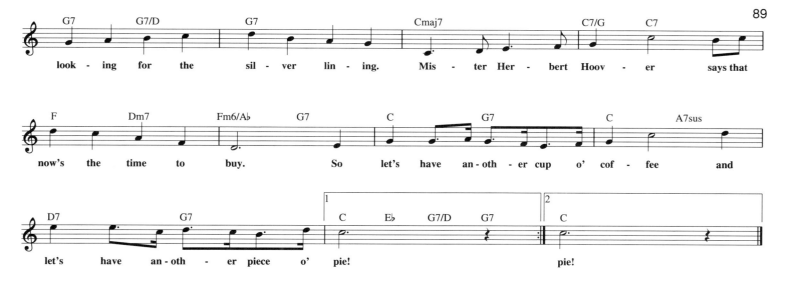

IT ONLY HAPPENS WHEN I DANCE WITH YOU
(From The Motion Picture Irving Berlin's EASTER PARADE)

© Copyright 1947 by Irving Berlin
© Copyright Renewed

Words and Music by
IRVING BERLIN

IT'S A LOVELY DAY TODAY
(From The Stage Production CALL ME MADAM)

Words and Music by
IRVING BERLIN

LET YOURSELF GO
(From The Motion Picture FOLLOW THE FLEET)

Words and Music by
IRVING BERLIN

© Copyright 1936 by Irving Berlin
© Copyright Renewed

Moderately

As you listen to the band don't you get a bubble? As you listen to them play don't you get a glow? If you step out on the floor you'll forget your trouble. If you go into your dance you'll forget your woe. So come, get together. Let the dance floor feel your leather. Step as lightly as a feather. Let yourself go. Come hit the timber. Loosen up and start to limber. Can't you hear that hot marimba? Let yourself go. Let yourself go, relax, and let yourself go. Relax, you've got yourself tied up in a knot. The night is cold, but the music's hot. So come, cuddle closer. Don't you dare to answer, "No Sir." Butcher, banker, clerk and grocer, let yourself go.

LITTLE FISH IN A BIG POND
(From The Stage Production MISS LIBERTY)

Words and Music by
IRVING BERLIN

Moderately

A lit-tle fish in a big pond has plen-ty of room to swim. But swim-ming a-round are big fish all rea-dy to pounce on him. Back to his lit-tle pond he starts to roam. The lit-tle fish spreads his fins and be-gins to swim back home. That's me, a lit-tle fish in a big pond, all wrong. That's me, a lit-tle fish where a lit-tle fish don't be long. A lit-tle man in a big town gets but-ter-flies in his dome. I'm rea-dy to spread my fin and be-gin to swim back home to the lit-tle pond, where a lit-tle fish and a lit-tle man be-long.

lit-tle fish in a big pond has got-ta have lots of heart. For swim-ming a-round are big fish but if he's the least bit smart. Back to his lit-tle pond he does-n't go. The lit-tle fish spreads his fins and be-gins to grow, grow, grow. That's you, a lit-tle fish in a big pond, all right, me too. A lit-tle fish, but we got-ta stand up and fight. A lit-tle man in a big town don't have to get out and roam. Stop tak-ing it on the chin and be-gin to feel at home in the big-ger pond, where the big-ger fish and the big-ger men be-long. A long.

MANDY
(From The Stage Productions YIP, YIP, YAPHANK, and ZIEGFELD FOLLIES Of 1919)

© Copyright 1919 by Irving Berlin
© Copyright Renewed by Irving Berlin
© Copyright Assigned to Joe DiMaggio, Anne Phipps Sidamon-Eristoff
and Theodore R. Jackson as Trustees of God Bless America Fund

Words and Music by
IRVING BERLIN

I was strolling out one evening. By the silv'ry moon, I could

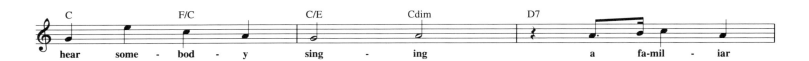
hear somebody singing a familiar

tune. So I stopped a while to listen, not a

word I wanted to miss. It was just somebody

serenading, something like this.

Mandy, there's a minister handy. And it sure would be

dandy, if we'd let him make a fee. So don't you

linger, here's the ring for your finger.

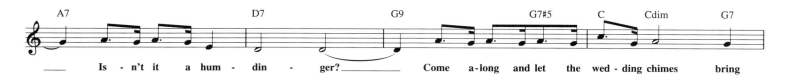
Isn't it a humdinger? Come along and let the wedding chimes bring

happy times, for Mandy and me. me.

ME

110

© Copyright 1931 by Irving Berlin
© Copyright Renewed

Words and Music by
IRVING BERLIN

MOONSHINE LULLABY
(From The Stage Production ANNIE GET YOUR GUN)

Words and Music by
IRVING BERLIN

Slow Blues Tempo

Be-hind the hill there's a bus-y lit-tle still where your Pap-py's work-ing in the moon-light. Your lov-in' Paw is-n't quite with-in the law, so he's hid-ing there be-hind the hill. Bye, bye ba-by. Stop your yawn-ing. Don't cry ba-by. Day will be dawn-ing. And when it does, from the moun-tain where he wuz he'll be com-ing with a jug of moon-shine. So count your sheep, Mam-ma's sing-ing you to sleep with the moon-shine lull-a-by. Dream of Pap-py, ver-y hap-py, with his jug of moun-tain rye. So count your sheep, Mam-ma's sing-ing you to sleep with the moon-shine lull-a-by.

KATE (HAVE I COME TOO EARLY, TOO LATE)

Words and Music by
IRVING BERLIN

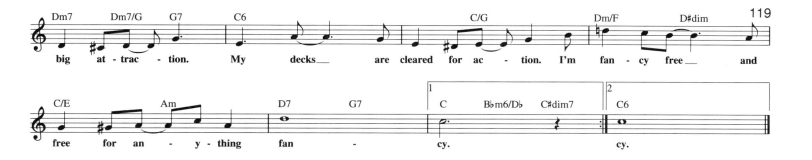

REACHING FOR THE MOON
(From The Motion Picture REACHING FOR THE MOON)

© Copyright 1930 by Irving Berlin
© Copyright Renewed

Words and Music by
IRVING BERLIN

NOW IT CAN BE TOLD
(From The 20th Century Fox Motion Picture ALEXANDER'S RAGTIME BAND)

© Copyright 1938 by Irving Berlin
© Copyright Renewed

Words and Music by
IRVING BERLIN

Freely

All the world's great lov-ers have been glo-ri-fied. Hist-'ry placed them in a ro-man-tic set. In be-tween book cov-ers they are side by side. But the real thing has-n't been writ-ten yet.

Slowly

Now it can be told, told in all its glo-ry. Now that we have met, the world may know the sen-ti-men-tal sto-ry. The great-est ro-mance they ev-er knew is wait-ing to un-fold. Now it can be told as an in-spi-ra-tion. Ev-'ry oth-er tale of "Boy meets Girl" is just an im-i-ta-tion. The great love sto-ry has nev-er been told be-fore, but now, now it can be told. told.

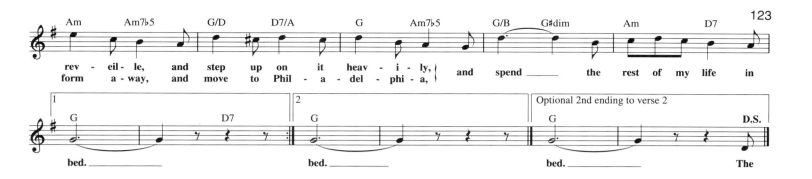

RUSSIAN LULLABY

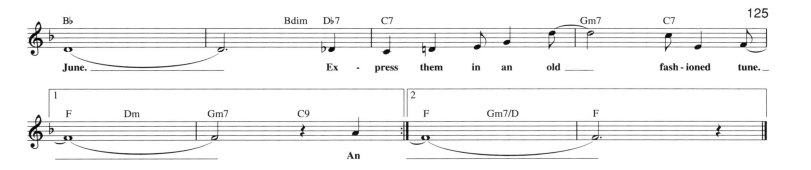

ONLY FOR AMERICANS
(From The Stage Production MISS LIBERTY)

© Copyright 1949 by Irving Berlin
© Copyright Renewed

Words and Music by
IRVING BERLIN

Brightly

On-ly for A-mer-i-cans _____ the mid-night life in gay Pa-ree. The French-man he would nev-er see, it's on-ly for A-mer-i-cans. _____ The pric-es in the smart ca-fé, the French-man he would nev-er pay. The price that's more is on-ly for A-mer-i-cans from the U. S. A. _____ A Mo-marte la-dy drops her hank-y and sly-ly winks her eye. That's on-ly for a Yan-kee, the French-man would-n't buy. On-ly for A-mer-i-cans _____ the French-men on the bou-le-vards don't buy those dirt-y pos-tal cards. They're on-ly

On-ly for A-mer-i-cans _____ the shops with man-y real an-tiques. An-tiques as old as sev-en weeks, they're on-ly for A-mer-i-cans. _____ The bed on which a King made love which there are sev-'ral doz-ens of. The French poo poo we sell them to A-mer-i-cans from the U. S. A. _____ Those old Na-pol-eon brand-y la-bles that re-cent-ly were made. They're not for French-men's ta-bles, they're for the Yan-kee trade. On-ly for A-mer-i-cans _____ the French-man gets his kiss-es free but those for which there is a fee, are on-ly

On-ly for A-mer-i-cans _____ a French-man's food is ver-y plain. The fan-cy sau-ces with pto-maine are on-ly for A-mer-i-cans. _____ A French-man sel-dom eats the snails with lit-tle ul-cers on their tails. And all that cheese was made to please A-mer-i-cans from the U. S. A. _____ While the A-mer-i-can ca-rous-es where crim-son sha-dows creep, the French a-void those hous-es. They go to bed to sleep. On-ly for A-mer-i-cans _____ the French-man would-n't be im-pressed to see a show with girls un-dressed. That's on-ly

On-ly for A-mer-i-cans _____ the French-men don't keep com-pa-ny with south of France so-ci-e-ty, that's on-ly for A-mer-i-cans. _____ The French-man has-n't large a-mounts to pay for Ba-rons, Dukes and Counts that you a-dore. They're on-ly for A-mer-i-cans from the U. S. A. _____ We like to keep the good re-la-tions that noth-ing must up-set. We give you de-cor-a-tions that French-men sel-dom get. On-ly for A-mer-i-cans _____ a our fin-est art is in the Louvre, the ones the ex-perts don't ap-prove are on-ly

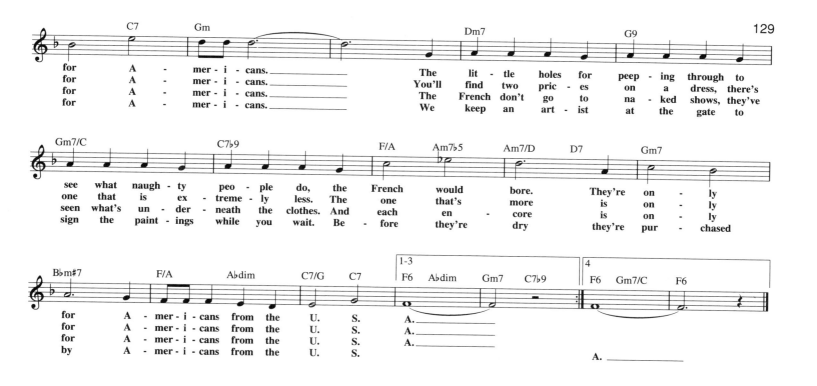

PARIS WAKES UP AND SMILES
(From The Stage Production MISS LIBERTY)

Words and Music by IRVING BERLIN

SAYONARA
(From The Motion Picture SAYONARA)

© Copyright 1953, 1957 by Irving Berlin
© Copyright Renewed

Words and Music by
IRVING BERLIN

A Pretty Girl Is Like A Melody
(From The 1919 Stage Production ZIEGFELD FOLLIES)

© Copyright 1919 by Irving Berlin
© Copyright Renewed

Words and Music by
IRVING BERLIN

I have an ear for mu-sic, and I have an eye for a maid. I like a pret-ty girl-ie, with each pret-ty tune that's played. They go to-geth-er, like sun-ny weath-er goes with the month of May. I've stud-ied girls and mu-sic, so I'm qual-i-fied to say: A pret-ty girl is like a mel-o-dy that haunts you night and day. Just like the strain of a haunt-ing re-frain, she'll start up-on a mar-a-thon and run a-round your brain. You can't es-cape she's in your mem-o-ry. By morn-ing, night and noon She will leave you and then come back a-gain. A pret-ty girl is just like a pret-ty tune. A pret-ty tune.

REMEMBER

Words and Music by
IRVING BERLIN

Moderate Waltz

One lit-tle kiss, a mo-ment of bliss, then hours of deep re-gret.
In-to my dreams you wan-dered it seems, and then of there came a day.

One lit-tle smile, and af-ter a while, a long-ing to for-get.
You loved me too, my dreams had come true, and all the world was May.

One lit-tle heart-ache left as a to-ken, one lit-tle play-thing care-less-ly bro-ken.
But soon the May-time turned to De-cem-ber. You had for-got-ten, do you re-mem-ber?

Re-mem-ber the night, the night you said "I love you," re-mem-ber? Re-mem-ber you vowed by all the stars a-bove you, re-mem-ber? Re-mem-ber we found a lone-ly spot, and af-ter I learned to care a lot, you prom-ised that you'd for-get me not. But you for-got to re-

To Coda

1. mem-ber. 2. Re-mem-ber.

D.C. al Coda

CODA

mem-ber.

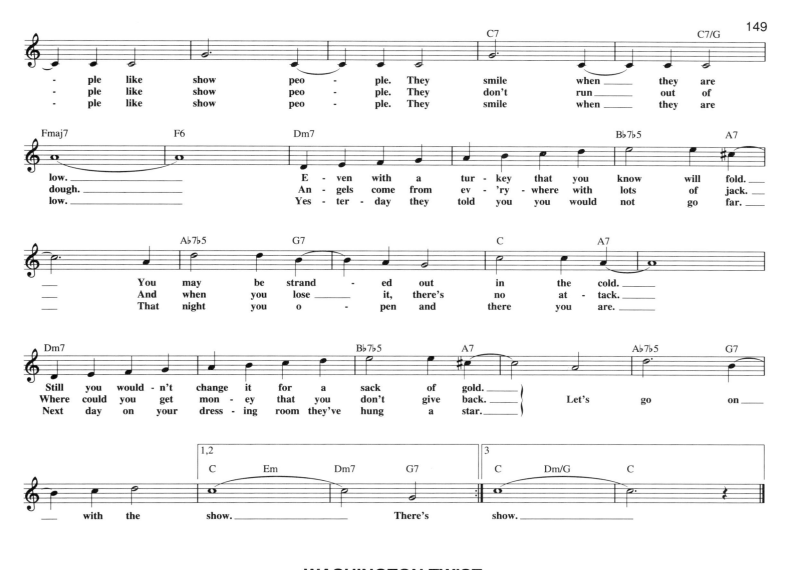

WASHINGTON TWIST
(From The Stage Production MR. PRESIDENT)

© Copyright 1962 by Irving Berlin
© Copyright Renewed

Words and Music by
IRVING BERLIN

THIS YEAR'S KISSES
(From The 20th Century Fox Motion Picture ON THE AVENUE)

© Copyright 1937 by Irving Berlin
© Copyright Renewed

Words and Music by
IRVING BERLIN

Slowly

I didn't cry when romance was through, _____ I looked around for somebody new. _____ Since my romance I've kissed one or two, _____ but I'm afraid their kisses won't do. _____

This year's crop of kisses don't seem as sweet to me. _____ This year's crop just misses what kisses used to be. _____ This year's new romance _____ doesn't seem to have a chance, _____ even helped by Mister Moon above. _____ This year's crop of kisses is not for me, _____ for I'm still wearing last year's love.

love. _____

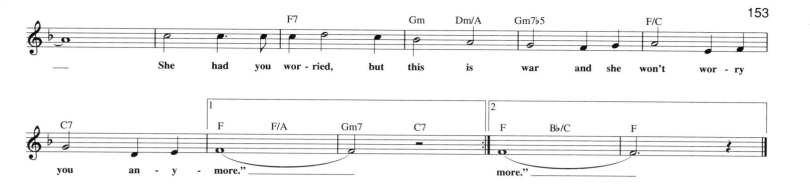

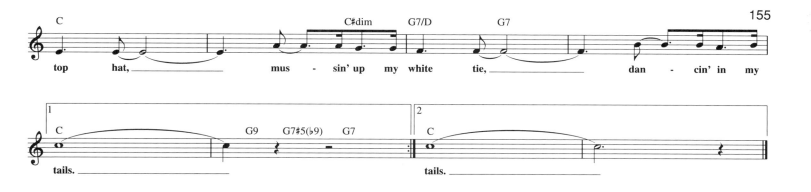

THE SONG IS ENDED
(BUT THE MELODY LINGERS ON)

Words and Music by
IRVING BERLIN

© Copyright 1927 by Irving Berlin
© Arrangement Copyright 1951 by Irving Berlin
© Copyright Renewed

WHAT CHANCE HAVE I WITH LOVE
(From The Stage Production LOUISANA PURCHASE And The Motion Picture Irving Berlin's CALL ME MADAM)

Words and Music by
IRVING BERLIN

Slowly, but rhythmically

Love is beau-ti-ful, love is swell. Love is as sweet as a nut.

Love is grand-er than tongue can tell. Love is re-mark-a-ble. But

look at what it did to An-thon-y. It made a fool out of An-thon-y. If

love could do that to An-thon-y, what chance have I with love?

Look at what it did to Ro-me-o. It dealt poor Ro-mey an aw-ful blow. If

love could do that to Ro-me-o, what chance have I with love?

Look what it did to Samp-son, 'til he lost his hair he was brave. If a

hair-cut could weak-en Samp-son, they could mur-der me with a shave.

Look at what it did to Bo-na-parte. He lost his head when he

lost his heart. If he kicked o-ver the ap-ple cart, what chance have I an

or-di-nar-y guy, what chance have I with love?

WHEN WINTER COMES
(From The Motion Picture Irving Berlin's SECOND FIDDLE)

Words and Music by
IRVING BERLIN

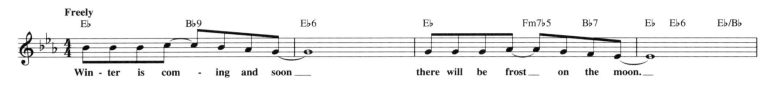
Win-ter is com-ing and soon there will be frost on the moon.

Snow will be fall-ing and what am I go-ing to do. I'll need some-bod-y to hold,

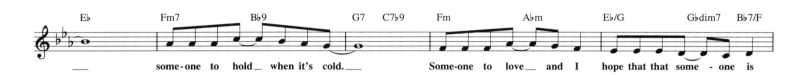
some-one to hold when it's cold. Some-one to love and I hope that that some-one is

you. The sun will shine in the sum-mer and I'll be fine in the sum-mer.

But then I've got-ta have you to cud-dle up to when win-ter comes.

It's nice and warm in the sum-mer. I'll be in form in the sum-mer.

But then I've got-ta have you to cud-dle up to when win-ter comes.

All sum-mer I'll be play-ing out on a ten-nis court.

But in the win-ter just like the ground-hog I'll turn in-

WHAT'LL I DO?

Words and Music by
IRVING BERLIN

Dedicated to General H.H. Arnold and the U.S. Army Air Forces

WITH MY HEAD IN THE CLOUDS
(From The Stage Production THIS IS THE ARMY)

Words and Music by
IRVING BERLIN

© Copyright 1942 by Irving Berlin
© Copyright Renewed by Irving Berlin
© Copyright Assigned to Joe DiMaggio, Anne Phipps Sidamon-Eristoff and
Theodore R. Jackson as Trustees of God Bless America Fund

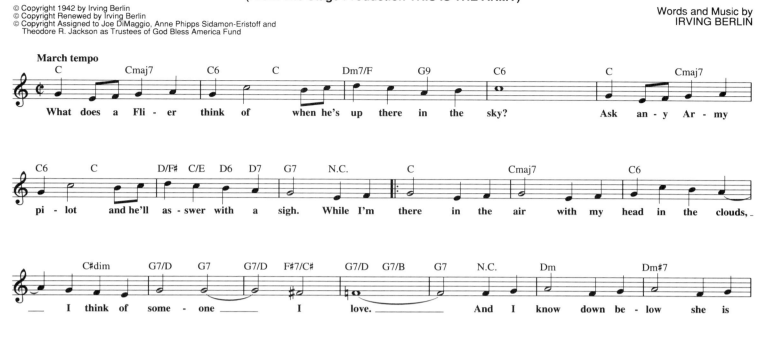

YOU CAN'T GET A MAN WITH A GUN
(From The Stage Production ANNIE GET YOUR GUN)

Words and Music by
IRVING BERLIN

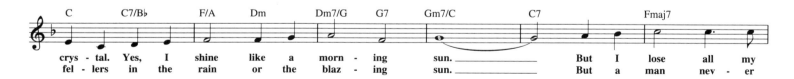

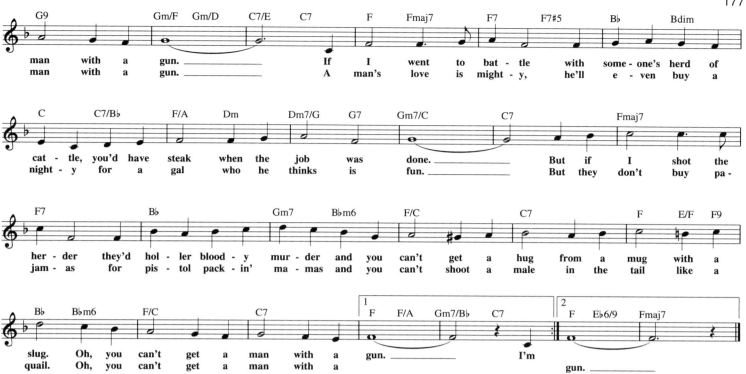

YOU'D BE SURPRISED

Words and Music by
IRVING BERLIN

© Copyright 1919 by Irving Berlin
© Arrangement Copyright 1958 by Irving Berlin
© Copyright Renewed

He's not so good in a crowd but when you get him a-lone, you'd be sur-prised.

He is-n't much at a dance but then when he takes you home, you'd be sur-prised.

He does-n't look like much of a lov-er, but don't judge a book by it's cov-

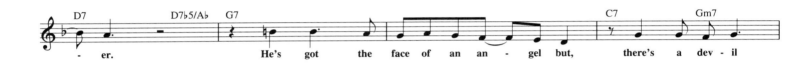
-er. He's got the face of an an-gel but, there's a dev-il

in his eye. He's such a del-i-cate thing but when he starts in to squeeze, you'd be sur-prised.

He does-n't look ver-y strong but when you sit on his knees, you'd be sur-prised.

At a par-ty or at a ball, I've got to ad-mit he's noth-ing at all, but in an

eas-y chair, you'd be sur-prised. He's not so